21 Prayers of Gratitude

Overcoming Negativity Through the Power of Prayer and God's Word

Shelley Hitz

21 Prayers of Gratitude

Published by Body and Soul Publishing
Printed In the United States Of America

ISBN-13: 978-1-946118-06-6

Table of Contents

21 Prayers of Gratitude

Prayer changes things. It changes me. When I pray consistently to God something changes within me. However, sometimes it is easy to get caught up in the busyness of life and not take the time to pray.

We do not have to pray in a certain way for God to hear us. We can simply lift up the prayer of our hearts to Him as if we are talking with a friend. However, in this book, I have taken key truths from scripture and reworded them into prayers of gratitude. Combining prayer with God's Word is powerful. I have experienced this in my own life and now want to share it with you.

They say it takes 21 days to form a new habit. And so I have shared 21 prayers of gratitude with you to help you form a habit of prayer in your life. I pray that these prayers help you to overcome negativity through applying the power of prayer and God's Word to your life. I also pray that when you finish this book, your prayers will continue on your own.

I encourage you to dig into God's Word and come up with your own prayers. If you are struggling in a certain area, I recommend using a concordance or an online tool like BibleGateway.com or BlueLetterBible.org to find scriptures on that topic and then reword them into prayers from your own heart.

Are you ready to get started? Let's start with a prayer...

Lord I thank You for each person who reads this book and lifts up these prayers to You. I pray that You would do a mighty work in their hearts as they spend these next 21 days in prayer with You. Change them from the inside out through Your Word and prayer. Give them a hunger and thirst for You that will continue past the last page of this book. We love You and thank You for this opportunity to come to You with our prayers of gratitude. Amen.

"Pray without ceasing."

- I Thessalonians 5:17

"Ask, and it will be given to you; seek, and you will find; knock, and it will be opened to you."

- Matthew 7:7

"Be anxious for nothing, but in everything by prayer and supplication, with thanksgiving, let Your requests be made known to God; 7 and the peace of God, which surpasses all understanding, will guard Your hearts and minds through Christ Jesus."
- Philippians 4:6-7

Prayer of Gratitude #1: Grace

Lord, today I want to thank You for Your grace. Grace is simply getting something good I do not deserve. So many times I take Your grace for granted, please forgive me. Open my eyes to see Your grace more clearly in my life. Lord, I ask that You take the blinders off of my spiritual eyes so that I can see all of the gifts You have so graciously given me.

It is by Your grace ALONE that I am saved from eternal punishment and have the promise that I will be with You in heaven for eternity one day. Thank You for rescuing me from my sin and from the clutches of the evil one, Satan. You died for me so that I could have life and life abundantly. Thank You for Your sacrifice.

Thank You for giving me life each new day. When I wake up in the morning, empower me to focus my first thoughts on You. As I lay my head on the pillow at night, remind me of all that You have given me that day. Show me the gifts You have given me and empower me to say a simple, "Thank You" back to You.

Thank You for Your amazing grace. Without it, I would be in a hopeless situation. But, because of

Your grace, I have so much to be thankful for today…and every day.
I love You, Lord.   Amen.

"Every good gift and every perfect gift is from above, and comes down from the Father of lights, with whom there is no variation or shadow of turning."

- James 1:17

"For by grace you have been saved through faith, and that not of yourselves; it is the gift of God."

- Ephesians 2:8

"The thief does not come except to steal, and to kill, and to destroy. I have come that they may have life, and that they may have it more abundantly.

- John 10:10

"May grace (God's favor) and peace (which is perfect well-being, all necessary good, all spiritual prosperity, and freedom from fears and agitating passions and moral conflicts) be multiplied to you in [the full, personal, precise, and correct] knowledge of God and of Jesus our Lord."

- 2 Peter 1:2 (AMP)

Prayer of Gratitude #2: New Beginnings

Lord, today I want to thank You for new beginnings. Your mercies are new every morning; great is Your faithfulness to me even when I turn my back on You. Sometimes I walk away from You deliberately through sin in my life. But many times, the distance between You and I is a slow fade, where I gradually spend less and less time with You.

And I can feel the difference.

When I spend quality time with You every day, I sense Your presence in my life and Your love, joy and peace. As I get busy and don't intentionally take time to be with You, I can feel a darkness settle over me. It may come in the form of worry, anxiety, self-pity, a complaining spirit or even sin.

Lord, forgive me for the times I have ignored You. You are walking with me each day and yet many times I do not acknowledge Your presence. I am so sorry. Empower me to change through Your Holy Spirit so that I can offer You the best part of my day, every day. Clearly show me how important my time with You is each day and allow me to make You a priority in my life, like I never have before.

Jesus, You knew how important time with Your Father was and often withdrew to a place so that You could be alone with Him. Many times this was early in the morning. Give me the willingness to make sacrifices to spend time with You, even if it means sacrificing sleep or giving up watching my favorite TV show or time on the internet.

I love You, Lord, and thank You for this fresh start today where I can make my relationship with You the biggest priority in my life. Amen.

"Through the Lord's mercies we are not consumed, Because His compassions fail not. They are new every morning; Great is Your faithfulness."
- Lamentations 3:22-23

"I am with you always, even to the end of the age."
- Matthew 28:20

"So He Himself often withdrew into the wilderness and prayed."
- Luke 5:16

"Immediately He made His disciples get into the boat and go before Him to the other side, to Bethsaida, while He sent the multitude away. And when He had sent them away, He departed to the mountain to pray."
- Mark 6:45-46

Prayer of Gratitude #3:
Unconditional Love

Lord, today I want to thank You for Your unconditional love. Nothing can separate me from Your love and yet many times I do not believe this truth from Your word, the Bible. I struggle to feel and understand Your unconditional love because I don't experience it anywhere else in my life. Others will always let me down or disappoint me at one time or another. No earthly person, aside from You, Jesus, is able to love me perfectly and unconditionally. And sometimes I project my earthly relationships onto You.

However, You are not like any of my other relationships. I can put my full trust in Your love and know that You will always be there for me and love me unconditionally, no matter what I do or what happens to me.

Empower me to grasp how high and deep and wide is Your love for me. Your love is not just a generic love for the entire world, but is also a very personal love directed to me as well. You love me. Let me repeat that to allow that truth to sink into my mind, heart and soul. You. Love. Me. And Your love knows no limits, bounds or conditions. Thank You, Lord, for Your unconditional love for me. Amen."

"For I am persuaded that neither death nor life, nor angels nor principalities nor powers, nor things present nor things to come, nor height nor depth, nor any other created thing, shall be able to separate us from the love of God which is in Christ Jesus our Lord."

- Romans 8:38-39

"For this reason I bow my knees to the Father of our Lord Jesus Christ, from whom the whole family in heaven and earth is named, that He would grant You, according to the riches of His glory, to be strengthened with might through His Spirit in the inner man, that Christ may dwell in Your hearts through faith; that You, being rooted and grounded in love, may be able to comprehend with all the saints what is the width and length and depth and height— to know the love of Christ which passes knowledge; that You may be filled with all the fullness of God.

Now to Him who is able to do exceedingly abundantly above all that we ask or think, according to the power that works in us, to Him be glory in the church by Christ Jesus to all generations, forever and ever. Amen."

- Ephesians 3:14-21

Prayer of Gratitude #4:
The Holy Spirit

Lord, today I want to thank You for the gift of the Holy Spirit in my life. Jesus, You said You had to go away so that the Helper, the Holy Spirit, would come. And now, because I have put my trust in You, this gift and access to the power of the Holy Spirit has been given to me.

I find it difficult to fully grasp and understand it all, but I thank You for equipping me and giving me the Holy Spirit. The Holy Spirit is my Counselor, Helper and Teacher. The Holy Spirit empowers me with supernatural strength and power to do things that I could not do on my own.

I am so thankful that I am never alone. Jesus, You walk with me, my Heavenly Father is always with me and I am empowered by the Holy Spirit. Thank You, Lord, for providing for me in so many ways.

I am sorry for the times that I have grieved the Holy Spirit in my life and instead have tried to live out of my own strength and power. Please forgive me. Help me to be sensitive to the Holy Spirit and to obey Your promptings in my life. I am so thankful that I do not have to live this life on my own. Thank You for providing what I need today. Amen.

"Nevertheless I tell you the truth. It is to your advantage that I go away; for if I do not go away, the Helper will not come to you; but if I depart, I will send Him to you. And when He has come, He will convict the world of sin, and of righteousness, and of judgment."

- John 16:7-8

"But the Helper, the Holy Spirit, whom the Father will send in My name, He will teach you all things, and bring to your remembrance all things that I said to you."

- John 14:26

"But you shall receive power when the Holy Spirit has come upon you; and you shall be witnesses to Me in Jerusalem, and in all Judea and Samaria, and to the end of the earth."

- Acts 1:8

"Then Peter said to them, 'Repent, and let every one of you be baptized in the name of Jesus Christ for the remission of sins; and you shall receive the gift of the Holy Spirit.'"
- Acts 2:38

Prayer of Gratitude #5:
Peace

Lord, today I want to thank You for Your peace that passes all understanding. In a world full of stress, anxiety and chaos; I am so thankful for Your peace in my life.

It is so easy for me to give in to feelings of anxiety throughout my day and I ask for Your forgiveness. Empower me to be changed by the renewing of my mind with Your peace and complete trust in You. Just as a young child does not hesitate, but jumps without fear into their father's arms, empower me to trust You fully and to fall into Your capable arms.

Instead of worrying about my circumstances, help me to develop the habit of bringing my concerns to You through prayer. Then, Your peace that passes all understanding will guard and protect my mind and heart.

I would never consider holding on to a grenade where the pin has been pulled and is ready to blow up. Instead, I would throw it as far away from me as possible. In the same way, help me to throw my stress and anxiety onto You. You can handle it…I cannot. When I hold on to my stress, it has the power to destroy me. Right now I visualize myself casting my burdens onto You. I ask You to instead fill me with Your peace through Your Holy Spirit.

Thank You for Your peace that calms my soul. I love You, Lord! Amen.

"Be anxious for nothing, but in everything by prayer and supplication, with thanksgiving, let your requests be made known to God; and the peace of God, which surpasses all understanding, will guard your hearts and minds through Christ Jesus."

- Philippians 4:6-7

"Lean on, trust in, *and* be confident in the Lord with all your heart *and* mind and do not rely on your own insight *or* understanding. In all your ways know, recognize, *and* acknowledge Him, and He will direct *and* make straight *and* plain your paths."

- Proverbs 3:5-6 (AMP)

"Casting the whole of your care [all your anxieties, all your worries, all your concerns, once and for all] on Him, for He cares for you affectionately and cares about you watchfully."

- I Peter 5:7 (AMP)

"But the fruit of the Spirit is love, joy, peace, longsuffering, kindness, goodness, faithfulness, gentleness, self-control. Against such there is no law."

- Galatians 5:22-23

Prayer of Gratitude #6: Guidance and Direction

Lord, today I want to thank You for the guidance and direction You give me every day through the Holy Spirit. Sometimes I wander off Your path and start doing what I think it best without consulting You. Please forgive me for making decisions apart from You. Empower me to change and put You at the center of everything I do.

You have promised to never leave me nor forsake me. You are with me every step of the way, every single day. When I am at a crossroads and do not know what to do, remind me to come to You first, even before my family and friends. Your guidance and direction is what I want more than anything else.

I am so thankful that You instruct me and teach me in the way I should go. I have experienced the promptings of the Holy Spirit that guide me and I know that You have my best interests in mind, even when the path gets difficult. You also guide me through Your word, the Bible. It is a lamp unto my feet and a light unto my path.

When I get stuck and don't know what to do, all I need to do is simply pray and ask You. You have promised to give me wisdom when I ask You for it. Thank You, Lord, for the way You lovingly lead and guide me each day. Open my ears so that I can hear Your still, small voice. Amen.

"I will never leave you nor forsake you."

- Hebrews 13:5b

"I will instruct you and teach you in the way you should go;   I will counsel you with my loving eye on you."

- Psalm 32:8 (NIV)

"Your word is a lamp to my feet and a light to my path."

- Psalm 119:105

"Whether you turn to the right or to the left, your ears will hear a voice behind You, saying, 'This is the way; walk in it.'"

- Isaiah 30:21 (NIV)

"If any of you lacks wisdom, let him ask of God, who gives to all liberally and without reproach, and it will be given to him. But let him ask in faith, with no doubting, for he who doubts is like a wave of the sea driven and tossed by the wind."

- James 1:5-6

Prayer of Gratitude #7:
Nature

Lord, today I thank You for the beauty of Your creation, nature. Your beauty surrounds me every day and I am reminded of You. Thank You for these simple gifts to enjoy each day.

- Flowers
- Sunsets
- Rivers
- Mountains
- Rainbows

And the list could go on and on. The beauty of Your creation amazes me and reminds me of Your creativity. Thank You for allowing me to enjoy Your creation each day no matter where I am. Whether I am walking along the beach, on a trail in a forest or along the sidewalk of a busy city – Your fingerprints are all around me.

I love the smells of nature as well: the fragrance after the rain, the sweetness of fresh flowers or the scent of pine trees.

May I never take Your creation for granted and thank You for the beauty You surround me with each day.

"The heavens declare the glory of God; the skies proclaim the work of his hands."

- Psalm 19:1

"The earth is the Lord's, and all its fullness, the world and those who dwell therein. For He has founded it upon the seas, and established it upon the waters."

- Psalm 24:1-2

"For by Him all things were created that are in heaven and that are on earth, visible and invisible, whether thrones or dominions or principalities or powers. All things were created through Him and for Him."

- Colossians 1:16

Prayer of Gratitude #8:
Hope

Lord, today I thank You for the hope I have in You. This life is not all there is and for that I am so thankful. Many people live for this life only; however, I know that there is so much more. Thank You that the best is yet to come in heaven.

Even though the hard days hit and dark times come on this side of heaven, I know that I can still hope. The enemy wants me to feel as if I am trapped inside a dark room without any doors to escape. However, You remind me that I am not trapped in a room, but simply walking through a tunnel. This too shall pass. Thank You for walking with me through the dark days and giving me hope even when I can't see the end.

Thank You for the hope of heaven. I look forward to seeing You face to face and being in a place where there will no longer be tears or pain. What a day it will be.

Your hope sustains me, Lord. Thank You for strengthening me with Your hope today. I love You. Amen.

"We give thanks to the God and Father of our Lord Jesus Christ, praying always for you, since we heard of your faith in Christ Jesus and of your love for all the saints; because of the hope which is laid up for you in heaven, of which you heard before in the word of the truth of the gospel."

- Colossians 1:3-5

"Now may the God of hope fill you with all joy and peace in believing, that you may abound in hope by the power of the Holy Spirit."

- Romans 15:13

"Blessed is the man who trusts in the Lord, and whose hope is the Lord,"

- Jeremiah 17:7

"Let us hold fast the confession of our hope without wavering, for He who promised is faithful."
- Hebrews 10:23

Prayer of Gratitude #9: Strength

Lord, today I thank You for the strength You give me. I feel weak and fragile today - and yet I know that when I am weak, You are strong. Infuse me with Your strength today.

Just as my cell phone needs recharged regularly, I need recharged as well. My recharging comes from spending time with You and I thank You that it can even be as simple as saying two words - "Jesus, help." You long to give me strength and to recharge me physically, emotionally and spiritually. Remind me often throughout my day of Your presence with me.

Lord, apart from You I can do nothing. And I feel it. When I try to do things in my own strength I get tired and overwhelmed very easily. But, when I am depending on Your strength, I can run and not grow weary. Thank You for giving me the strength I need to face whatever comes my way today. I love You. Amen.

"Therefore I take pleasure in infirmities, in reproaches, in needs, in persecutions, in distresses, for Christ's sake. For when I am weak, then I am strong."

-2 Corinthians 12:10

"I am the vine; you are the branches. If you remain in me and I in you, you will bear much fruit; apart from me you can do nothing."

- John 15:5 (NIV)

"But those who wait on the Lord shall renew their strength; They shall mount up with wings like eagles, they shall run and not be weary, they shall walk and not faint."

- Isaiah 40:31

Prayer of Gratitude #10: Protection

Lord, today I want to thank You for Your protection over my life. I thank You that when I put my trust in You, You will be my shield and my refuge. You are my hiding place and protect me from trouble.

There is evil all around me and I can feel the spiritual battle every day. And yet, You are my protector and You shield me from the enemy. This does not mean that I will never experience trouble in this life, but it does mean that You will be with me and that in the end You will overcome. You are a strong tower and when I run to You, Jesus, I am safe.

I claim Your promise today that says "no weapon formed against me shall prosper." I command any evil spirits to leave me in Jesus name and thank You for the blood of Jesus that covers me and protects me from the evil one. Thank You for Your protection over me physically, emotionally and spiritually today. Amen.

"You are my hiding place; You shall preserve me from trouble; You shall surround me with songs of deliverance."

- Psalm 32:7

"The name of the Lord is a strong tower; the righteous run to it and are safe."

- Proverbs 18:10

"No weapon formed against you shall prosper, and every tongue which rises against you in judgment you shall condemn. This is the heritage of the servants of the Lord, and their righteousness is from Me," says the Lord."

- Isaiah 54:17

"But the Lord is faithful, and he will strengthen you and protect you from the evil one."

- 2 Thessalonians 3:3 (NIV)

*See also Psalm 91.

Prayer of Gratitude #11:
Healing

Lord, today I want to thank You for Your healing power in my life. I have experienced Your healing in many ways: spiritually, emotionally and physically. You have come to heal the broken hearted and I thank You for the emotional healing You have brought into my life. There are days that are still difficult, but I know that You are walking with me and that I am not alone. It takes time and patience as You heal me stitch by stitch, but it is worth it.

Thank You for Your healing power that is available to my physical body as well. Jesus, when You walked this earth, one of the ways You demonstrated Your power was to bring physical healing to many…and You continue to do so today. I realize that Your healing may look differently than I expect and I will choose to trust You even when I don't understand all the "why's."

I praise You that I am fearfully and wonderfully made and that You place Your healing hand upon my life each and every day. I love You. Amen.

"The Spirit of the Lord God is upon Me, because the Lord has anointed Me to preach good tidings to the poor; He has sent Me to heal the brokenhearted, to proclaim liberty to the captives, and the opening of the prison to those who are bound."

- Isaiah 61:1

"Yea, though I walk through the valley of the shadow of death, I will fear no evil; for You are with me; Your rod and Your staff, they comfort me."

- Psalm 23:4

"And Jesus went about all Galilee, teaching in their synagogues, preaching the gospel of the kingdom, and healing all kinds of sickness and all kinds of disease among the people."

- Matthew 4:23

"I will praise You, for I am fearfully and wonderfully made; Marvelous are Your works, And that my soul knows very well."

- Psalm 139:14

Prayer of Gratitude #12:
The Body of Christ

Lord, today I want to thank You for the body of Christ, other believers You have placed in my life. Just as my physical body is designed to work together with all of its parts functioning properly, Your Church, the body of Christ is intended to work together as well.

Thank You for the people You strategically place in my life to encourage me when I need it the most. This encouragement may come in the form of encouraging words, a prayer or even a simple smile. Many times I can feel Your love through other believers.

I realize that apart from Jesus, no human being is perfect this side of heaven. Therefore, there will be issues that arise sometimes within the Church. I ask Your forgiveness for the times that I have given into a spirit of gossip, judgment or division. Please forgive me. You long for there to be a spirit of unity and love amongst the body of Christ. I pray that Your love would flow through me to other believers within the Church and that You would show me how to be an encouragement and support to them. Use me as Your light wherever I go. Amen.

"Just as a body, though one, has many parts, but all its many parts form one body, so it is with Christ."

- I Corinthians 12:12 (NIV)

"Two are better than one, because they have a good reward for their labor. For if they fall, one will lift up his companion. But woe to him who is alone when he falls, for he has no one to help him up. Again, if two lie down together, they will keep warm;

But how can one be warm alone? Though one may be overpowered by another, two can withstand him. And a threefold cord is not quickly broken."

- Ecclesiastes 4:9-12

"Beloved, let us love one another, for love is of God; and everyone who loves is born of God and knows God."

- I John 4:7

"I do not pray for these alone, but also for those who will believe in Me through their word; that they all may be one, as You, Father, are in Me, and I in You; that they also may be one in Us, that the world may believe that You sent Me.

- John 17:20-21

Prayer of Gratitude #13: Faithfulness

Lord, today I want to thank You for Your faithfulness. Even when I am unfaithful to You, You are always faithful to me. Great is Your faithfulness.

Amidst a world of changes, You are a God who never changes. You are the same yesterday, today and forever. Even when others' opinions of me change, when the economy changes, when the fashion trends change; You never change. Thank You for being the solid rock in my life that I can always depend on.

I thank You, Lord, that You are faithful in ALL You do. I admit that sometimes I don't understand Your ways. But I know that just as a Polaroid picture is fuzzy at first and then later fully develops and is seen clearly, I too will someday see things clearly. You will either reveal it to me later in this life or I will fully understand once I reach heaven. Help me to put my trust in Your faithfulness in the midst of the "fuzziness" of my life.

I am so grateful that You are faithful to forgive my sins when I confess them to You. Your faithfulness touches my life in so many ways. Great is Your faithfulness! Amen.

"Through the Lord's mercies we are not consumed, because His compassions fail not. They are new every morning; great is Your faithfulness."

- Lamentations 3:22-23

"Jesus Christ is the same yesterday, today, and forever."

- Hebrews 13:8

"For the word of the Lord is right and true; He is faithful in all He does."

-Psalm 33:4 (NIV)

"If we confess our sins, He is faithful and just to forgive us our sins and to cleanse us from all unrighteousness."

- I John 1:9

Prayer of Gratitude #14:
The Bible

Lord, today I am thankful for Your Word, the Bible, which You use to speak to me. Your Word is a lamp unto my feet and a light unto my path. When I feel confused and not sure what to do, I can look to Your Word which will guide me and lead me.

I am thankful that You chose to inspire men to write down Your words. You are the author; they were merely the vessels You used. I praise You that the Bible has been so well preserved through the years so that it could be passed down to us today.

Lord, help me to never take the Bible for granted. Give me a renewed passion and thirst for Your Word and to know You better through it. As I read it, memorize it and study it; I am getting to know You in a deeper way - the creator of this universe. Thank You that You choose to make Yourself known to me in many ways including the Bible.

And as the grass withers and the flowers fade away, I praise You that Your Word stands FOREVER!! Amen.

"Your word is a lamp to my feet and a light to my path."

- Psalm 119:105

"For prophecy never came by the will of man, but holy men of God spoke as they were moved by the Holy Spirit."

- 2 Peter 1:21

"All Scripture is given by inspiration of God, and is profitable for doctrine, for reproof, for correction, for instruction in righteousness."

- 2 Timothy 3:16

"The grass withers, the flower fades, but the word of our God stands forever."

- Isaiah 40:8

Prayer of Gratitude #15:
Faith

Lord, thank You that You are not only the author of my faith but also the perfecter of my faith. I ask that You continue to perfect my faith as many times I still waver in unbelief. I confess my unbelief to You right now. As the father said to Jesus about healing his son, "I do believe; help me overcome my unbelief." I ask Your forgiveness and pray for the strength to believe in You despite my circumstances.

I also realize that without faith it is impossible to please You. Impossible. Help me to remember this when doubts slip into my mind and lies from the enemy tempt me to not believe Your promises. Strengthen me with power from Your Holy Spirit to have faith that stands the test of time.

Thank You for equipping me with the shield of faith to fight the battles that wage in my mind. With my shield of faith raised high, I can quench the fiery darts from the enemy that seek to destroy me.

And right now I affirm my faith and belief in You, Lord. I believe, I believe, I do believe! Amen.

"Let us fix our eyes on Jesus, the author and perfecter of our faith, who for the joy set before him endured the cross, scorning its shame, and sat down at the right hand of the throne of God." (NIV)

- Hebrews 12:2

"Immediately the boy's father exclaimed, 'I do believe; help me overcome my unbelief!'"

- Mark 9:24 (NIV)

"But without faith it is impossible to please Him, for he who comes to God must believe that He is, and that He is a rewarder of those who diligently seek Him."

- Hebrews 11:6

"Above all, taking the shield of faith with which you will be able to quench all the fiery darts of the wicked one."

- Ephesians 6:16

Prayer of Gratitude #16: Laughter and Joy

Lord, today I want to thank You for laughter. A deep belly laugh truly is medicine for the soul. Laughter is an expression of joy and I long to experience Your joy in my life each day. I realize that joy is different than happiness. Happiness is dependent on happenings and my circumstances whereas I find joy in You.

I ask that You help me to have child-like faith so that I can find joy in each day. There is nothing better than seeing a child's face light up with a smile and laugh at the smallest things in life. They find joy in everyday life. Help me to be filled with Your Holy Spirit and Your joy, as one of the fruit of Your Spirit is joy. I thank You that in Your Presence is fullness of joy!

However, I admit that sometimes my feelings are up and down. Some days I don't feel like laughing and that's okay too. There is a season for everything: a time to laugh and a time to cry; a time to grieve and a time to dance. Even when I am walking through dark and difficult times, You are with me and You comfort me. Thank You Lord that even in the difficult days, Your joy can be my strength. Amen.

"A cheerful heart is good medicine, but a crushed spirit dries up the bones."

- Proverbs 17:22 (NIV)

"But the fruit of the Spirit is love, joy, peace, longsuffering, kindness, goodness, faithfulness, gentleness, self-control. Against such there is no law."

- Galatians 5:22-23

"You will show me the path of life; in Your presence is fullness of joy; at Your right hand are pleasures forevermore."

- Psalms 16:11

"To everything there is a season, a time for every purpose under heaven…a time to weep, and a time to laugh; a time to mourn, and a time to dance."

- Ecclesiastes 3:1, 4

"Yea, though I walk through the valley of the shadow of death, I will fear no evil; for You are with me; Your rod and Your staff, they comfort me."

- Psalm 23:4

"Do not sorrow, for the joy of the Lord is Your strength."

- Nehemiah 8:10b

Prayer of Gratitude #17:
Spiritual Gifts

Lord, today I want to thank You for the spiritual gifts You have given me. There are many different spiritual gifts, but they all come from You. Thank You that You give gifts to every one of us within the body of Christ, including myself. No one has been left empty handed. Even if the gifts You have given me do not seem as important as another person's, they are essential to the body of Christ, the Church. Just as my intestines are as important as my eyes in my physical body, You created the Church to work together with the gifts You have given us in unity.

I pray that You would continue to reveal to me what my spiritual gifts are…some are apostles, prophets, evangelists, pastors and teachers. And yet You've also given us gifts of prophesy, serving, encouragement, giving and leading. And these are just a few of the gifts You have given us. Next, empower me to use the gifts You've given to me. Help me to be obedient to use my gifts no matter how insignificant they may seem.

I also thank You when someone uses their gifts to bless me. Thank You for those that have taught me Your Word, given generously to me, served me and encouraged me. Thank You for using others in powerful ways in my life. Amen.

"There are diversities of gifts, but the same Spirit. There are differences of ministries, but the same Lord. And there are diversities of activities, but it is the same God who works all in all."

- I Corinthians 12: 4-6

"But in fact God has placed the parts in the body, every one of them, just as he wanted them to be. If they were all one part, where would the body be? As it is, there are many parts, but one body."

- I Corinthians 12:18-20 (NIV)

"And He Himself gave some to be apostles, some prophets, some evangelists, and some pastors and teachers, for the equipping of the saints for the work of ministry, for the edifying of the body of Christ"

- Ephesians 4:11-12

"We have different gifts, according to the grace given to each of us. If your gift is prophesying, then prophesy in accordance with your faith; if it is serving, then serve; if it is teaching, then teach; if it is to encourage, then give encouragement; if it is giving, then give generously; if it is to lead, do it diligently; if it is to show mercy, do it cheerfully."

- Romans 12:6-8 (NIV)

Prayer of Gratitude #18:
Self Control

Lord, today I want to thank You for self-control. As Your child, I have access to Your Holy Spirit. And the fruit of the Holy Spirit is self-control. I thank You for providing me with everything I need; however, I confess that sometimes I lack self-control. I ask for Your forgiveness today. Fill me anew with Your Spirit and Your self-control for every situation I will face.

Sometimes it feels like temptation has overtaken me, but You promise to be faithful and always provide a way of escape. Empower me to take Your way of escape when You offer it to me. Thank You Lord that I can have victory over temptation and self-control when I am empowered by Your Spirit. May I walk in that victory today. Amen.

"But the fruit of the Spirit is love, joy, peace, longsuffering, kindness, goodness, faithfulness, gentleness, self-control. Against such there is no law."

- Galatians 5:22-23

"No temptation has overtaken you except such as is common to man; but God is faithful, who will not allow you to be tempted beyond what you are able, but with the temptation will also make the way of escape, that you may be able to bear it."

- I Corinthians 10:13

"For God gave us a spirit not of fear but of power and love and self-control."

- 2 Timothy 1:7 (ESV)

Prayer of Gratitude #19:
Freedom

Lord today I want to thank You for the freedom in Christ You have given me. Through Christ, You have given me freedom from the sin that so easily entangles me. I have been a prisoner to sin and chained down by heavy weights. Thank You for forgiving me and lifting the weight of my sin off of me.

Thank You for helping me to stand firm in this freedom I have in Christ. Help me not to be burdened again by the regret and shame of my past but empower me to walk in the freedom You have given me. One way I can do this is by putting Your truth, Your Word, into my mind each day. When I know Your truth, it will set me free.

Another way I can stand firm in the freedom You have given me is to come to You daily and confess my sins to You. This keeps me unburdened and free. Bring to my mind any sin I need to confess to You right now. I take this moment to confess these sins to You: _____ (stop and confess your sins to God). Thank You for Your forgiveness. I ask that You empower me to truly change and repent. I love You Lord and I thank You for the freedom You have given me today. Amen.

"Therefore, since we are surrounded by such a great cloud of witnesses, let us throw off everything that hinders and the sin that so easily entangles. And let us run with perseverance the race marked out for us."

- Hebrews 12:1

"It is for freedom that Christ has set us free. Stand firm, then, and do not let yourselves be burdened again by a yoke of slavery."

- Galatians 5:1 (NIV)

"Then Jesus said to those Jews who believed Him, "If you abide in My word, you are My disciples indeed. And you shall know the truth, and the truth shall make you free."

- John 8:31-32

"Therefore if the Son makes you free, you shall be free indeed."

- John 8:36

"The Spirit of the Sovereign Lord is on me, because the Lord has anointed me to proclaim good news to the poor. He has sent me to bind up the brokenhearted, to proclaim freedom for the captives and release from darkness for the prisoners."
- Isaiah 61:1 (NIV)

Prayer of Gratitude #20: Patience

Lord today I want to thank You for patience. Patience is definitely not something that comes naturally to me but is a supernatural gift from Your Spirit. Thank You for equipping me with patience for people and circumstances in my life. Many times, things do not happen the way I plan or in the timing I would like. I surrender my desire to control the people and happenings in my life to You. Help me to have Your patience and contentment even when my circumstances do not change.

Waiting on You is hard. But, ultimately I know that Your timing is best. Give me the ability to see life through Your perspective, an eternal perspective. I want to love others with Your love, a love that is patient and kind. However, I know that I cannot do it on my own strength and that I need Your empowerment to change.

I love You Lord. Even when I am waiting on You and do not see any changes, I trust You with the details of my life. Amen.

"But the fruit of the Spirit is love, joy, peace, longsuffering, kindness, goodness, faithfulness, gentleness, self-control. Against such there is no law."

- Galatians 5:22-23

"Rest in the Lord, and wait patiently for Him."

- Psalm 37:7a

"Love is patient, love is kind. It does not envy, it does not boast, it is not proud."

- I Corinthians 13:4 (NIV)

"And let us not grow weary while doing good, for in due season we shall reap if we do not lose heart."

- Galatians 6:9

Prayer of Gratitude #21: Salvation

Lord today I want to thank You for my salvation. I know that without You, I would have no hope beyond this life. For I have sinned against You in so many ways and my sin separates me from You. Thank You that You have given me the gift of eternal life through the sacrifice Jesus made on the cross. So many misunderstand You...You did not send Jesus to condemn the world, but to save it. I pray that my unsaved relatives and friends would come to truly know You and trust in Jesus for their salvation. For when we confess with our mouths that Jesus is Lord and believe in our hearts that You raised him from the dead, we will be saved.

I thank You that salvation is truly a gift from You, nothing I can earn by doing good works or trying harder. Faith without works is dead, but ultimately salvation comes only as a gift from You.

I praise You that I am a new creation – the old has passed away and the new has come. Thank You for changing my heart and my life...I am forever grateful to You. Help me to share my relationship with You with others. Amen.

"For all have sinned and fall short of the glory of God."

- Romans 3:23

"For the wages of sin is death, but the gift of God is eternal life in Christ Jesus our Lord."

- Romans 6:23

"For God so loved the world that He gave His only begotten Son, that whoever believes in Him should not perish but have everlasting life. For God did not send His Son into the world to condemn the world, but that the world through Him might be saved."

- John 3:16-17

"That if you confess with your mouth the Lord Jesus and believe in your heart that God has raised Him from the dead, you will be saved."

- Romans 10:9

"For by grace you have been saved through faith, and that not of yourselves; it is the gift of God."

- Ephesians 2:8

"Thus also faith by itself, if it does not have works, is dead."

- James 2:17

"Therefore, if anyone is in Christ, he is a new creation; old things have passed away; behold, all things have become new."

- 2 Corinthians 5:17

21 Stories of Gratitude

"If you look at the world, you'll be distressed. If you look within, you'll be depressed. But if you look at Christ, you'll be at rest."

- Corrie ten Boom

What a great quote by one of my heroes of the faith, Corrie ten Boom. She was a Nazi prison camp survivor and knew what it was like to go through difficult circumstances in life. However, as we share in one of the stories later in this book, Corrie and her sister Betsie found out that it is possible to live life with a grateful heart. They displayed gratitude even when living amongst some of the worst circumstances we can imagine.

How about you? Are you living life to the fullest? Or are you merely surviving from day to day?

One way to live life to the fullest is to live each day with a grateful heart. In this book, we share 21 stories of gratitude to give you encouragement and hope in your own journey. Gratitude is possible! Even though many times we cannot change our circumstances, we can change the way we see them. We can ask God to empower us to change our thoughts. Beth Moore explains this well in a quote from her Patriarchs study, *"I have been told many times, 'Beth, I can't change the way I feel.' But we can change the way we think, which will lead to a*

45

change in the way we feel. That's the essences of the renewed mind."

Our prayer for you is that you find encouragement within these pages. And we pray that you will ask God for His strength to renew your mind with His truth and the hope He offers each one of us every day. It is only through Christ renewing our minds that we can truly live each day with a grateful heart.

"And do not be conformed to this world, but be transformed by the renewing of your mind, that you may prove what is that good and acceptable and perfect will of God."

Romans 12:2 (NKJV)

Story of Gratitude #1:
Changed From Within

Heather Hart

"Let the peace of Christ rule in your hearts, since as members of one body you were called to peace. And be thankful."

Colossians 3:15 (NIV)

When I first began thinking of a gratitude story to share, I honestly could not think of one. However, after some prayerful contemplation I realized that the reason I could not think of a specific way

46

gratitude has impacted my life, was because it has done so in such a complete way.

You see, several years ago I went through a Revive Our Hearts 30-Day Husband Encouragement Challenge. While I don't remember them ever using the word gratitude to describe what they were teaching us, that is exactly what I got out of it. They encouraged us to not say anything negative to our husbands or about our husbands for 30 days - thus they encouraged us to choose gratitude.

This was in the first years of my marriage. My husband and I were raising four children together, two boys from a previous marriage and our newborn twin girls. As only one of the four was old enough for school, I had to quit my job and become a full time stay at home mommy - there simply were not any jobs that could pay enough to cover the cost of day care for three children - and I was miserable. The only adult I ever saw was my husband. He was coming home from working 12 hour shifts at his job, exhausted, only to encounter a wife that was stressed to the max, and looking for someone to blame and take over. Looking back, I most certainly don't envy what he went through, and have been thanking God ever since for saving my marriage.

Throughout the 30-days of learning to be grateful for my husband, not only did my marriage improve, but my walk with God grew to an entire new level. I started seeing Him in a new way. He wanted me to choose gratitude and thank Him for what He had blessed me with - even when the twins were crying. Even when I hadn't slept for more than an hour at a time in the past 3 months. Even when my husband wasn't reading my mind. Even when the house was a disaster.

Choosing gratitude helped me to see things in a whole new light. It was no longer about where I was, or what was happening in the moment. It was about what I had, and what God had done for me. No, my husband is not perfect, but neither am I. My kids don't always listen, and my house still isn't clean - but God has taught me to be grateful for my life anyway. To be thankful for my wonderful children, and that we have a place to live.

I still have days where the depression sinks in, but God always brings me back to His peace and reminds me of what He has given me. Moreover, even when I'm in the throes of life, I am grateful that my family and my God love me enough to stick with me through it all.

This was an excerpt from the eBook, "*21 Stories of Gratitude: The Power of Living Life With a Grateful Heart.*"

Continue Reading

Continue reading on gratitude in my book, "A Life of Gratitude." Not only does it have 21 stories of gratitude, but it contains a 21 day gratitude journal.

Get it here:
www.bodyandsoulpublishing.com/gratitudeprint

Our prayer for you is that you find encouragement within these pages. And we pray that you will ask God for His strength to renew your mind with His truth and the hope He offers each one of us every day. It is only through Christ renewing our minds that we can truly live each day with a grateful heart.

Get your here:
www.bodyandsoulpublishing.com/21stories

A Life of Gratitude: 21 Days to Overcoming Self-Pity and Negativity (Print)

Get all three of the best-selling books in the gratitude series in one print book.

Get your print copy at:
www.bodyandsoulpublishing.com/gratitudeprint

My Scripture Journal: Gratitude

Dig deeper in your gratitude walk with "My Scripture Journal: Gratitude." "My Scripture Journal: Gratitude" is an eight week Bible memory reading plan designed to help You memorize scripture while also offering guidance so You can dive further into a greater knowledge of what the Bible says about gratitude. Get started with this eight week reading plan and download to Your Kindle for just $0.99 today!

www.bodyandsoulpublishing.com/gratitudejournal

Get Free Christian Books

Love getting FREE Christian books online? If so, sign up to get notified of new Christian book promotions and never miss out. Then, grab a cup of coffee and enjoy reading the free Christian books you download.

You will also get our FREE report, "*How to Find Free Christian Books Online*" that shows You 9 places you can get new books…for free!

Sign up at:
www.bodyandsoulpublishing.com/freebooks

Happy reading!

CJ and Shelley Hitz

CJ and Shelley Hitz enjoy sharing God's Truth through their speaking engagements and their writing. On downtime, they enjoy spending time outdoors running, hiking and exploring God's beautiful creation.

To find out more about their ministry, go to www.ShelleyHitz.com.

Note from the Author: Reviews are gold to authors! If you have enjoyed this book, would you consider reviewing it on Amazon.com? Thank you!

Other Resources from Shelley Hitz

For Writers

Shelley is an author coach and has resources for writers and authors

Writing Week: a free 7-day writing challenge. Get started here: www.writingweek.com

Free Training: get all her free training for authors here: www.shelleyhitz.com/free

For Artists

Shelley teaches online art classes in lettering and watercolor for beginners.

Get started with 3 free classes here: www.yourcreativeadventure.com/free